UNOFFICIAL
GUIDES
JUNIOR

Starter Guide to
Rocket League

TRAIN
CHALLE
Complete the Basic Tut
Playlist

Play 1 Online Match

Get 1 Shot on Goal in

VIEW CHA

by Josh Gregory

CHERRY LAKE PRESS
Ann Arbor, Michigan

Published in the United States of America by Cherry Lake Publishing
Ann Arbor, Michigan
www.cherrylakepublishing.com

Reading Adviser: Beth Walker Gambro, MS, Ed., Reading Consultant, Yorkville, IL

Photo Credits: Images by Josh Gregory

Cherry Lake Press is an imprint of Cherry Lake Publishing Group.

Library of Congress Cataloging-in-Publication Data has been filed and is available at catalog.loc.gov

Printed in the United States of America by
Corporate Graphics

Note from the Publisher: Websites change regularly, and their future contents are outside of our control. Supervise children when conducting any recommended online searches for extended learning opportunities.

Contents

Powerful Fun!

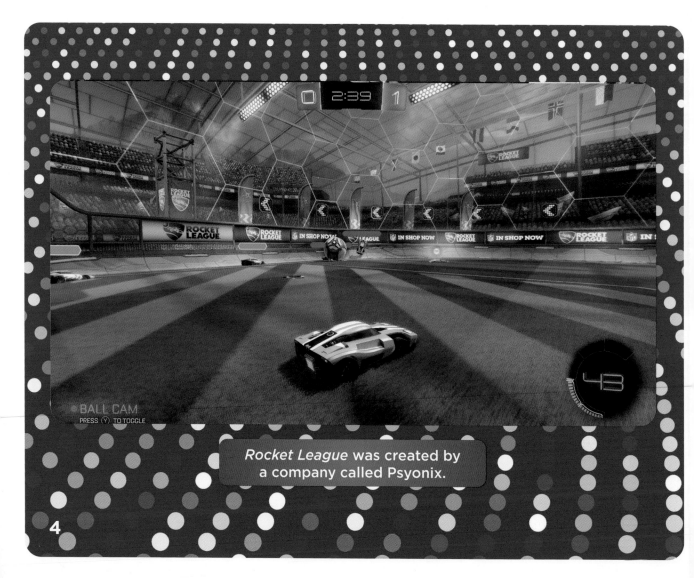

Rocket League was created by a company called Psyonix.

Did you know there's a video game about cars and soccer? The idea is simple. Players use cars to hit a huge soccer ball into a goal. The game is called *Rocket League*! It came out in 2015. Today, it's enjoyed by millions of players.

Free to Play

In 2020, *Rocket League* was made free to play. This means that anyone can download it and start playing!

Ready to Play

At the start of each match, cars race to get the ball.

When you play *Rocket League* for the first time, there's a video to watch. It explains the basic controls of the game. These include how to **accelerate**, jump, and boost your car. The car, however, isn't ordinary. It's rocket-powered!

Basic Rules

Multiple people can play *Rocket League* at the same time.

The basic rules of *Rocket League* are easy. There are two teams. Matches can be one-on-one or as many as four-on-four. Each match is 5 minutes long. It begins with a big soccer ball in the field. Then teams try to knock the ball into the other's goal. The team with the most goals wins.

Tutorials

Rocket League has built-in **tutorials** to help you master the game. To access them, enter Training mode and select "tutorials" from the menu.

Eyes on the Ball

BALL CAM
PRESS SPACEBAR TO TOGGLE

4:16

When the ball is in the air, keep an eye on the circle on the ground. It will help you figure out where the ball will land.

To play well, you must keep your eyes on the ball. Arrows around your car help you do so. And when the ball is in the air, you'll see a target on the ground. It shows you where the ball will fall. Also, be sure to collect any glowing boost items. They will help you in many ways, such as going faster.

Scoring Goals

BALL CAM
PRESS Ⓐ TO TOGGLE

Time your speed boosts just right to reach the ball.

Scoring a goal isn't as easy as it looks. Try not to crowd the ball. Plan your goal. For example, instead of using your speed boost, save it. Use it to reach the ball at the right moment. Also, learn all of your car's moves. One move is the powerslide. It will assist you in scoring.

Jumping

Performing a double jump is a cool trick. To do this, jump again once you're already in the air. You can also boost your car in the air. If done right, your car will fly!

Off the Wall

Riding up the walls can help you get a better angle for your shots.

Did you know you can drive your car up the walls? If you're fast enough, you may reach the ceiling! This can help you travel from one side of the arena to the other. If you time it right, you can even hit a flying ball as you fall from the ceiling.

Teamwork

Good teamwork often leads to victory.

As you play, it's **crucial** to help your team. If you aren't sure how, remember to protect your goal. Any time the ball heads your way, hit it back toward the other team. Playing **defensively** can help win a match. Also, try to play with the same friends. That way, you'll learn their play styles.

Team Chat

Chat as you play! Open the quick chat menu. You can plan moves. Only use voice chat with friends you know in real life. If you're playing with strangers, use quick chat.

Custom Cars

Players can enhance their cars using
Rocket League's in-game store.

Rocket League players can **customize** their cars! You can earn points called XP. Collecting XP allows players to level up something called a Rocket Pass. Then you can unlock custom wheels, decals, toppers, and more.

Rocket Pass

There are two versions of the Rocket Pass. One is free and the other is not. The paid version offers more custom items. It also increases the rate at which players gain XP. Talk to an adult before you spend money on any game!

What's Next?

Backspace Reset Ball
1 Take Possession
2 Start Dribble
3 Pass Ball
4 Launch Ball
5 Defend Shot

It's time to start exploring the world of *Rocket League*!

If this all sounds exciting, it is! *Rocket League* has tons of ways to customize your car. You can create something truly unique. Pick a car that suits you. Then get out there and start scoring goals.

Even Better

The team at Psyonix is always working to improve the game. They fix **bugs** in the game. They also add new car types and game modes.

GLOSSARY

accelerate (ak-SELL-uh-rayt) increase in speed

bugs (BUHGS) errors in a computer program's code

crucial (KROO-shuhl) critical or important

customize (KUHS-tuh-mahyz) to build according to certain specifications

defensively (dih-FEN-siv-lee) in a way that resists an attack

tutorials (too-TOR-ee-uhlz) instructions on how to play a game

FIND OUT MORE

BOOKS

Gregory, Josh. *Careers in Esports*. Ann Arbor, MI: Cherry Lake Publishing, 2021.

Loh-Hagan, Virginia. *Video Games. In the Know: Influencers and Trends*. Ann Arbor, MI: 45th Parallel Press, 2021.

Orr, Tamra. *Video Sharing. Global Citizens: Social Media*. Ann Arbor, MI: Cherry Lake Press, 2019.

Reeves, Diane Lindsey. *Do You Like Getting Creative? Career Clues for Kids*. Ann Arbor, MI: Cherry Lake Press, 2023.

WEBSITES

With an adult, learn more online with these suggested searches:

Rocket League
The official *Rocket League* home page is a great source for the latest news and updates about the game.

Rocket League Wiki
Check out this fan-made website for highly detailed, in-depth info about every aspect of *Rocket League*.

INDEX

ABOUT THE AUTHOR

Josh Gregory is the author of more than 200 books for kids. He has written about everything from animals to technology to history. A graduate of the University of Missouri–Columbia, he currently lives in Chicago, Illinois.